The Lesso

Smith

Wigglesworth

on

Faith

The Lessons of Smith Wigglesworth on *Faith*

LARRY KEEFAUVER,
GENERAL EDITOR

CREATION HOUSE
Orlando, FL

THE LESSONS OF SMITH WIGGLESWORTH ON FAITH
A Charisma Classics Bible Study
Larry Keefauver, General Editor
Published by Creation House
Strang Communications Company
600 Rinehart Road
Lake Mary, Florida 32746
Web site: http://www.creationhouse.com

Unless otherwise noted, all Scripture quotations are from the
King James Version of the Bible.

Scripture quotations marked NLT are from the Holy Bible,
New Living Translation, copyright © 1996.
Used by permission of Tyndale House Publishers, Inc.,
Wheaton, IL 60189. All rights reserved.

Contents

Introduction

WELCOME TO this devotional study guide on *The Lessons of Smith Wigglesworth on Faith.* This study guide is a companion volume to *The Original Smith Wigglesworth Devotional.*

This devotional study is part of a series of four Bible study guides focused on the teachings of some of the founding leaders of the Spirit-filled and Pentecostal movements—Smith Wigglesworth, John G. Lake, Maria Woodworth-Etter, and William J. Seymour from Azusa Street. Do not feel that you must go through this series in any particular order. Choose the guide and sequence that best meet your spiritual needs.

Just a word about Smith Wigglesworth: Smith Wigglesworth, the humble, anointed servant of God who dramatically shaped the early Pentecostal and Holiness movements on the continent and in the States, was called a twentieth-century apostle. Wigglesworth became a legend as God used him in an evangelistic, healing ministry. Born in 1859 in Menston, Yorkshire, England, he was converted in a Wesleyan Methodist meeting at age eight and pursued a career in plumbing. He married Polly Featherstone, and he and Polly operated a little mission in Bradford, England.

In 1907, in Sunderland, the forty-seven-year-old Wigglesworth received the baptism of the Holy Spirit, which radically changed him and transformed his ministry into a worldwide phenomenon. Literally thousands were saved, and untold scores were healed by God's power as Wigglesworth preached powerful messages power as Wigglesworth preached powerful messages throughout the world. He went home to the Lord he loved in 1947 at the age of eighty-seven.

This devotional study guide may be used by individuals, groups, or classes. A leader's guide for group or class sessions is provided at the end of this devotional study for those using this guide in a group setting. Groups using this guide should complete their devotional studies prior to their group sessions. This will greatly enhance sharing, studying, and praying together.

Individuals going through this guide can use it for daily devotional reading and study. The purpose of this guide is to help the reader(s) understand faith through the Scriptures with the insights of Smith Wigglesworth. All of the insights quoted from Smith Wigglesworth's precise words are placed between lines and italicized for easy recognition. Each daily devotional study is structured to:

❖ Probe deeply into the Scriptures.
❖ Examine one's own personal relationship in faith with Jesus Christ.
❖ Discover biblical truths about faith.
❖ Encounter Jesus Christ as personal Lord and Savior.

It is our prayer that as you study about faith daily in this devotional study that your life will be empowered by the Holy Spirit to trust Jesus Christ in every aspect of your life.

Day 1

The Measure of Faith

Now faith is the substance of things hoped for, the evidence of things not seen.

—Hebrews 11:1

I BELIEVE THERE IS *only one way to all the treasures of God, and that is the way of faith.*[1]

It does not take a great measure of faith on our part to give God the substance He requires to create a miracle. Jesus taught, "If ye have faith as a grain of mustard seed, ye shall say unto this mountain, Remove hence to yonder place; and it shall remove; and nothing shall be impossible to you" (Matt. 17:20).

What measure of faith do you have today? Put an *x* on the line that represents your faith:

_____

No Faith   Mustard Seed   Great Faith

Faith means "to trust." The one way to all the treasures of God is to trust Jesus Christ as your personal Lord and Savior. Read John 14:6, and then complete the following sentences:

I first trusted Jesus _____.

Each day I trust Jesus to _____.

> Y OU GET TO *know God by an open door of grace. He has made a way. It is a beautiful way that all His saints can enter in and find rest. The way is the way of faith. There isn't any other way.*[2]

You cannot earn your salvation. You need God's mercy to be saved.

Mercy is God's not giving us what we have earned. What have we earned? Judgment, sin, and death. Read Romans 5:12–14 and 6:23. In one sentence, describe what we have earned by our own efforts:

_____

_____

Grace is God's giving us what we have not earned. Read the following scriptures, and jot down what we receive in grace by faith in Christ:

John 3:16 _____

_____

Romans 5:15–17 _____

_____

Romans 6:23 _____

_____

Ephesians 2:8–9 _____

_____

BELOVED, I SEE *all the plan of life where God comes in and vindicates His power by making His presence felt. It is not by crying, nor groaning. It is because we believe. And yet, we have nothing to say about it. Sometimes it takes God a long time to bring us through the groaning and crying before we can believe.*[3]

Whatever measure of faith we have, God refines and purifies it through trials and fire. Often before our faith touches the power and presence of God, we must endure suffering.

Read 1 Peter 1:7–8, and then paraphrase it with your own words written in the fire below:

Pray . . .

Jesus, I believe in You. I trust You. I ask You to purify my faith beyond my groans, cries, and impatience to the pure gold of complete trust and surrender to You. Amen.

Day 2

Overcoming Faith

And this is the victory that overcometh the world, even our faith.

—1 JOHN 5:4

HRIST IS THE *root and source of our faith. When He is in what we believe for, it will come to pass. No wavering. This is the principle: He who believes is definite. A definite faith brings a definite experience and a definite utterance.*[4]

Faith is not *what* we believe; it's *who* we believe. True faith can never be focused on beliefs or creeds. Rather, faith centers in the person of Jesus the Christ (John 3:14–18). Below is a cross. On the cross write down all the different ways you trust Jesus as your Lord and Savior.

S OUR PRAYERS *rest upon the simple principle of faith, nothing shall be impossible to us.*[5]

With God, all things are possible—nothing is impossible. Read the following passages, and jot down what they reveal about all that is possible through faith in God:

Matthew 17:20

Matthew 19:26

Mark 10:27

Luke 1:37

Luke 18:27

What impossible things do you face for which you need faith in Christ who does the impossible? When you have done all that is possible, you enter the realm of the impossible. That territory belongs to God and can only be traversed by faith. Are you facing the impossible in your life? Check the areas of your life that seem to have impossible problems:

- ❏ Finances
- ❏ Family or marriage
- ❏ Spiritual life
- ❏ Other: _____

- ❏ Sickness and illness
- ❏ Job, career, or business
- ❏ Relationships

Now circle every area that you will totally trust Jesus to be Lord over in your life.

---

*T*HE ROOT PRINCIPLE *of all this divine overcoming faith in the human heart is Christ. When you are grafted deeply into Him, you may win millions of lives to the faith. Jesus is the Way, the Truth, and the Life, the secret to every hard problem in your heart.*[6]

Decide to trust Jesus with your life and all your problems. Only faith in Him can overcome the impossible in your life.

Pray . . .

Lord Jesus, I trust You with all of me and all of my impossible problems. You alone can do the impossible. Amen!

Day 3

𝕭𝖊𝖑𝖎𝖊𝖛𝖊 𝕿𝖍𝖆𝖙 𝕲𝖔𝖉 𝕴𝖘 𝕲𝖗𝖊𝖆𝖙𝖊𝖗

So then faith cometh by hearing, and hearing by the word of God.

—ROMANS 10:17

ON'T STUMBLE AT *the Word. Believe that God is greater than you are, greater than your heart, greater than your thoughts. Only He can establish you in righteousness even when your thoughts and your knowledge are absolutely against it.*[7]

Reason cannot comprehend the *will, ways,* and *when* of God. Remember that God's best is always greater than your best. God's idea is always greater than yours. God's ways are always greater than yours. And God's when, or timing, is always better than yours.

Identify the things in your life that you still hold onto that you think of as great hindrances. They may be your problems, failures, past sins, or enemies. Rank how greatly they attack you from the *greatest* (1), to the *least* (5).

_____ Problems
_____ Failures
_____ Past sin and guilt
_____ Enemies
_____ Other

Now name your greatest obstacle, burden, or bondage in life. Write it in the blank below:

_____

God is greater than my_____.

Say the above sentence over and over again until it moves out of your thoughts and into your heart.

HE WORD OF *God is true. If you will understand the truth, you can always be on line to gain strength, overcome the world, and make everything subject to you.*[8]

No matter what you think or perceive, God's Word is always true in spite of your experience or circumstances. God's Word is true at all times, for all people, and in all places. Read Psalm 119, and then list some of the benefits you will experience from trusting God's Word:

_____

_____

_____

God's Word will never fail you. His promises are forever true. You can trust your life with His Word. Decide to overcome the world around you by trusting God's Word.

Pray . . .

Lord, I trust Your Word to be a lamp to my feet and a light to my path. Amen.

Day 4

Faith Is a Gift

For by grace are ye saved through faith; and that not of yourselves: it is the gift of God.

—EPHESIANS 2:8

HUMAN FAITH WORKS *and then waits for the wages. That is not saving faith. Then there is the gift of faith. "For by grace are ye saved through faith; and that not of yourselves: it is the gift of God." Faith is that which God gave you to believe. "Whosoever believeth that Jesus is the Christ is born of God" (1 John 5:1).*[9]

Some people merely have faith in faith. They believe that if they believe strong enough, then something will happen. The fact is that true, genuine faith is a gift from God who empowers our faith through His Spirit. God provides us with *what* to believe, and then gives us the *power* to believe. What has God given you to believe? Complete the sentences below:

I Believe . . .

God is _____.

Jesus is _____.

The Holy Spirit is _____.

The Bible is _____.

Salvation is _____.

The church is _____.

If your beliefs are not God-given and God-empowered, then they are of natural faith, not divine faith.

E READ IN *1 Corinthians 12:9, "To another faith by the same Spirit." When my faith fails, then another faith lays hold of me. One time I thought I had the Holy Ghost. Now I know the Holy Ghost has got me. Human faith fails, but the faith of Jesus never fails.*[10]

When your faith begins to waver, what do you do? Rank from one (1) to (5) five the order of steps you take to bolster your faith:

_____ Seek God's face
_____ Pray
_____ Read the Word of God
_____ Encourage myself in the Lord
_____ Receive edification from other believers

If your faith is failing, then your faith is not rooted in God. His faith never fails. Read the following passages on faith's certainty, and jot down what they say to you about faith.

Romans 5:1–2 _____

_____

Romans 10:8–9 _____

2 Corinthians 8:7 _____

2 Corinthians 10:15 _____

Galatians 3:6–9 _____

Colossians 2:7 _____

Hebrews 11:1–2 _____

Stop trusting with your own strength and natural ability. Begin trusting in God's strength working in and through you.

𝔓𝔯𝔞𝔶 . . .

Lord Jesus, fill me with faith, and empower that faith. Amen.

Day 5

Two Kinds of Faith

Wherefore also we pray always for you, that our God would . . . fulfill all the good pleasure of his goodness, and the work of faith with power.
—2 Thessalonians 1:11

THERE ARE TWO *kinds of faith that God wants us to see. There is a natural faith, and there is a saving faith. All people are born with the natural faith. Natural faith has limitations. Saving faith is a supernatural gift of God. There is the gift of faith. It is the faith of Jesus given to us as we press in and on with God.*[11]

Imagine your walk of faith as running a race. Put an *x* on the line that indicates where you are right now:

Sprinter _____ Marathoner

Out of breath _____ Running smooth

Not focused _____ Fixed on Jesus

Impatient to finish _____ Running with patience

Too weak to go on _____ Finishing strong

Supernatural faith endures. It actually becomes stronger in trials and tests. Read 1 Peter 1:7–9, and summarize in your own words how your faith will be strengthened as you endure difficulties:

_____

_____

_____

A S I SAW *in God's presence the limitation of my natural faith, there came another faith, a supernatural faith that could not be denied, a faith that took the promise of God, a faith that believed God's Word.*[12]*

Being in God's presence always convicts us of our limitations in the natural. So in the natural, what are you tempted to trust? Check the boxes that apply to you.

❏ My own strength
❏ My relationships
❏ My job
❏ My friends
❏ My abilities and giftings
❏ My experience
❏ My intellect and knowledge

Once we let go of natural faith, we are free to grasp supernatural faith. Supernatural faith trusts the promises of God no matter how impossible the present circumstances may seem.

What does God promise? Read each of the following verses, and jot down a promise from God that you can trust absolutely:

The Word	God's Promise to You
Luke 24:49	
Acts 1:4–5, 2:23	
Galatians 3:14	
Ephesians 1:13–14	
Hebrews 9:15	
James 1:2	

Pray . . .

Lord, help me to let go of natural faith that I might grasp supernatural faith and trust completely Your promises. Amen.

Day 6

Faith Tried by Fire

That the trial of your faith . . . though it be tried with fire, might be found unto praise and honor and glory at the appearing of Jesus Christ.

—1 PETER 1:7

G OLD PERISHETH. *Faith never perisheth. It is more precious than gold, though it be tried by fire.*[13]

What fire does God use to try your faith? Trials of suffering and persecution rarely come against us like the sufferings faced by the early Christians, or believers who were persecuted under Stalin, Mao Tse Tung, Hilter, or Idi Amin. Still, each believer faces trials and tests.

Circle the areas in which your faith in Christ is now under attack:

Marriage   Family   Finances
Health   Church   Career
Education   Work   Relationships
Other: _____

When you face trial by fire, how do you usually respond? Rank your response to fire from *most often* (1), to *least often* (10):

_____ Fear
_____ Anger
_____ Discouragement
_____ Frustration
_____ Self-pity
_____ The desire to quit
_____ Hope
_____ Joy
_____ Excitement
_____ Desire to grow in faith

If you found yourself ranking more negative things than positive ones, then it's time for you to have an attitude adjustment. Read Philippians 2, and describe the attitude that Christ had toward suffering:

_____

_____

BELOVED, AS YOU *are tested in the fire, the Master is cleaning away all that cannot bring out His image, cleaning away all the dross from your life, all the evil, until He sees His face reflected in your life.*[14]

What is the Master cleaning away in your life? On the picture of soap below, write all the things that the Master is scrubbing from your life right now:

The purifying of our faith by fire is never pleasant or welcomed, but it is necessary for our spiritual growth in faith. Untried faith will never withstand the attacks of the enemy. The trials you now face will strengthen you to face greater challenges in the future. God is preparing you to be an overcomer, not just a survivor.

Pray . . .

Lord, purify my faith by the fire of trials, suffering, and tests. Strengthen me so that I may be an overcomer, not a victim, when I face future difficulties. Amen.

Day 7

Living Faith

Therefore if any man be in Christ, he is a new creature: old things are passed away; behold, all things are become new.

—2 CORINTHIANS 5:17

NOW THE HEART *cries out for a living faith with a deep vision of God. The world cannot produce it. Living faith is a place where we seek the Word, so that when we pray we know God hears. Living faith comes into the presence of God, asking Him and believing Him for the answer, while having no fear.*[15]

Living faith asks, seeks, and knocks. For what are you asking, seeking, and knocking? Examine your list. Read Luke 11:9–13. When you desire His presence, His Holy Spirit, then you will receive all that you need. Why settle for less? Through the Spirit comes every good gift. Stop seeking the *gifts* and instead seek the *Giver*—the Holy Spirit.

Write a prayer seeking, asking, and knocking so that the door will open for you to receive His Holy Spirit.

_____

_____

_____

I T IS OUR HUMAN *spirit that has to be controlled by the Holy Spirit. This world is full of stimulation. It is by faith, into a place of grace that all may see us anew. Behold! Behold! Behold! What is it? The Holy Ghost is arousing our attention. He has something special to say. Behold, if you will believe, you can be sons of God in likeness, character, spirit, and actions.*[16]

The Holy Spirit transforms us into new creations. When we seek Him by faith, we are changed into the likeness of Christ. Read 2 Corinthians 3:17–18. What does our new nature look like? The fruit of the Spirit is Christ's likeness revealed in us. Below are the fruit of the Spirit. Shade in each graph to the degree that quality of Christ is revealed in your new nature:

	Not evident							**Fully evident**
Love	/	/	/	/	/	/	/	/	/
Joy	/	/	/	/	/	/	/	/	/
Peace	/	/	/	/	/	/	/	/	/
Longsuffering	/	/	/	/	/	/	/	/	/
Gentleness	/	/	/	/	/	/	/	/	/
Goodness	/	/	/	/	/	/	/	/	/
Faith	/	/	/	/	/	/	/	/	/

Pray . . .

Lord Jesus, fill me with a living faith that trusts You to change, renew, and transform me into Your likeness. Amen.

Day 8

Only Believe

*As soon as Jesus heard the word that was spoken, he
saith unto the ruler of the synagogue, Be not afraid,
only believe.*

—MARK 5:36

---

*Only believe, only believe.
All things are possible, only believe.
Only believe, only believe.
All things are possible, only believe.*

THE IMPORTANCE *of that chorus is the word* only *right in the
midst of the chorus. If I can get you to see that when you get
rid of yourself, all human help, and everything else, and have
only God behind you, you have reached a place of great reinforce-
ment and continual success.*[17]

What keeps you from *only believing* in Christ? Check
below every hindrance to your faith:

❑ Unbelief   ❑ Busyness
❑ Strife   ❑ Anger
❑ Hopelessness   ❑ Impatience
❑ Depression   ❑ Insecurity
❑ Past failure and sin
❑ Other: _____

Faith in Christ does not depend on *self*—but on *Him.*
He is able to do in us what we could never do. But self must
be crucified (Gal. 2:20). Below is a nail representing

be crucified (Gal. 2:20). Below is a nail representing Christ's Crucifixion. On the nail, write the aspects of yourself or of your pride that need to be crucified:

_____   _____

_____   _____

_____

*I*F YOU HELP *yourself, to the measure you help yourself, you will find there are limitations to the life and power of God in you. The one grand plan God has for us is only believe. Absolute rest. Perfect submission. God has taken charge of the situation. You are absolutely brought into everything God has, because you dare only believe what He says. God would have me press into your heart a living truth: Only believe!*[18]

Read the following passages, and then list five benefits of faith in your life (Rom. 5:1–2; 1 Cor. 2:5; 2 Cor. 1:24; Gal. 2:16, 20; Eph. 2:8):

1. _____

2. _____

3. _____

4. _____

5. _____

Pray . . .

Almighty God, grant me the courage to set aside myself to only believe in You. Amen.

Day 9

Faith Acts

In the beginning was the Word, and the Word was with God, and the Word was God.

—JOHN 1:1

WE ARE SAVED BY *faith and kept by faith. Faith is a substance. It is also an evidence. God is. He is! Faith goes on to act. It's a reality, a deposit of God, an almighty flame moving you to act, so that signs and wonders are manifest.*[19]

Faith takes action. More than mental assent, faith believes, trusts, surrenders, commits, and follows. Jesus invites us to take action when we place our faith in Him. Read each of the following texts, and write down the corresponding action that Jesus desires you to take:

The Faith Action

Matthew 11:12 _____

Matthew 22:37–39 _____

Matthew 29:19 _____

Mark 2:9 _____

Mark 16:15 _____

Luke 11:9 _____

Faith moves us to action. James writes about how faith and action work together. Read James 1:22–27, and paraphrase in your own words the actions that faith inspires:

_____

_____

_____

---

*F*AITH TAKES YOU *to the place where God reigns, where you are imbibing God's bountiful store. Unbelief is sin.*[20]

It is impossible to say by faith, "Jesus is Lord," and then to say, "No, Lord." Faith moves us to obedience. If we truly believe He is Lord, then the only response we can make to His will is, "Yes, Lord." Not to obey Him is unbelief, rebellion, and sin.

In what areas of your life do you need to act in faith and say, "Yes, Lord!"? Check all that apply:

❏ My thought life   ❏ My feelings
❏ My attitudes   ❏ My habits
❏ My beliefs   ❏ My speech
❏ Other: _____

Faith does not put God first, it puts Him *only.* Our loyalty, priorities, and goals in life are on a list of one—God. He will not share your trust or faith with any other. Are you willing to make Him the only Lord in your life?

Pray . . .

Lord Jesus, I worship, serve, and trust only You. Amen.

Day 10

The Author of Faith

Looking unto Jesus the author and finisher of our faith.
—HEBREWS 12:2

E IS THE *author of faith. Jesus became the author of faith. God worked this plan through Him by forming the worlds, by making everything that there was by the word of His power. Jesus was the Word; Christ.*[21]

Jesus had much to say about faith in His teachings. Discover some of what He taught by reading the following scriptures and writing down what Jesus said about faith:

Matthew 8:9–10 _____

_____

Matthew 9:22 _____

_____

Matthew 17:20 _____

_____

Mark 11:22–23 _____

_____

Luke 18:41–43

Luke 22:31–32

As the author of our faith, Jesus . . .

❖ Inspires our faith by His Spirit.
❖ Empowers our faith to be strong, enabling us to stand firm.
❖ Renews our faith.
❖ Convicts and empowers us to act upon our faith.

Looking at the statements above, circle what Jesus is doing with your faith right now, and underline what you need Him to do most in your faith.

─────────────────────────────

GOD'S DIVINE PRINCIPLE *is that God hath chosen Jesus, ordained Him, clothed Him, and made Him greater than all because of the joy given by the love of God. Because of this exceeding, abundant joy of saving the whole world, He became the author of a living faith.*[22]

─────────────────────────────

Through Jesus Christ, God authors a living faith within us. That faith is filled with love and joy. Reflect for a moment on how your faith in Christ fills you with abundant love and joy. Complete these sentences:

My faith in Christ fills me with His love for _____

_____ .

My faith in Christ fills me with His joy for _____

_____ .

Jesus authors a *living* faith in you. How? Because He is life, trusting Him fills you with His life. Because His words are life, trusting and obeying His words brings you life. Ultimately, your faith is living because Jesus is alive!

Write a prayer thanking Jesus for infusing life into your faith and into you:

_____

_____

_____

Pray . . .

Lord Jesus, fill me with Your living and vital faith. Amen.

Day 11

Righteousness by Faith

*And be found in him, not having mine own right-
eousness . . . but . . . the righteousness which is of God
by faith.*

—PHILIPPIANS 3:9

OH, IF I *could, by God's grace, pour into you the difference
between our everyday righteousness and that attitude of a living
faith that dares claim and believe in Him! For I perceive there is
something after the righteousness of faith that you can never get by
the righteousness of the Law.*[23]

When you are clothed in His righteousness, a boldness
in faith comes into you that inspires you to believe for
signs and wonders in His name. What is righteousness? It
is being put into a right relationship with God through the
blood of Jesus Christ. Jesus becomes your righteousness.

Ephesians 6:14 reveals that in God's armor we have a
breastplate of righteousness and a shield of faith. Our
faith in Christ puts us in a position of protection behind
His righteousness.

On the next page is a shield of faith. On it, write all
the ways you have experienced the protection of His
righteousness in your walk with Him:

FAITH

ABRAHAM BELIEVED *God, and it was counted unto him for right-eousness. It was an imputed condition. God came forth and said to all the demons in hell and all the men on the earth, "Touch not that man." You can count on God to bring you through on all lines, for "no weapon that is formed against thee shall prosper" (Isa. 54:17).*[24]

God puts you in a position where the enemy cannot defeat you. Imagine a battle in which you are put on the front lines. There you are fully exposed to the attack of the enemy and subjected to great dangers. God never exposes you to danger. The blood of Christ protects you when you trust Jesus as Lord and Savior.

Therefore, having faith in Christ means you never have to defend yourself. He is your sure defense. Read the following passages, and then write down how faith in Christ is your sure defense:

1 Samuel 17:47 _____

_____

Psalm 28:7 _____

_____

Psalm 59

Romans 8:31

Romans 8:37–39

1 Corinthians 15:54–58

1 John 2:1–2

𝔓𝔯𝔞𝔶 . . .

Lord Jesus, by faith I put on Your breastplate of righteousness and seek Your protection from the enemy's fiery darts behind the shield of faith. Amen.

Day 12

Faith's Victory

*Above all, taking the shield of faith, wherewith ye shall
be able to quench all the fiery darts of the wicked.*
—EPHESIANS 6:16

REMEMBER THAT *God our Father intensely desires for us to have
all the full manifestation of His power so that we need nothing
but His Son. We have perfect redemption. We have all the power
of righteousness. We have to understand that we are brought into line
with all of God's power, dethroning the power of the enemy.*[25]

Faith releases the power of God in our lives. We need
no other power but His power to defeat the enemy. Read
Zechariah 4:6, and then write it in your own words:

_____

_____

_____

The enemy wants to keep you faithless and powerless.
Satan tempts Christians with doubt and unbelief so that
he can keep them powerless. Think about it. Satan knows
that the lost are already powerless, so he spends very little
energy attacking them. But power-filled Christians can
thwart the enemy at every turn. On the following list,
check the powerful weapons you use against the enemy,
and circle those you need to start using:

- ❏ The Word of God
- ❏ Prayer
- ❏ The armor of God
- ❏ The unity of the believers
- ❏ Confessing faith in Christ
- ❏ Other: _____

---

*I*F YOU ARE *afflicted in any way, do not for a moment, under any circumstances, come to the conclusion that the devil has enmity against you. No, he never has. The devil has nothing against you. But the devil is against the living Christ and wants to destroy Him. If you are filled with the living Christ, the devil is anxious to get you out of the way, thereby destroying Christ's power.*[26]

Satan is not out to get you. He is coming against the Christ who indwells you. You are Christ's vessel for sharing the gospel with the lost and for ministering to the "least of these." If the devil can render you powerless, then Christ cannot use you for the kingdom of God.

Check the ways listed below that Satan is using to try to get you out of the way:

- ❏ Depression
- ❏ Insecurity
- ❏ Condemnation
- ❏ Unbelief
- ❏ Fear
- ❏ Pride
- ❏ Other: _____

Satan cannot hinder the Spirit's work unless he weakens and debilitates God's people. He will use any attack to render helpless the people of God. When you are under his attack, what countermeasures do you take?

Circle all that apply:

Pray   Confess the Word   Give up
Cry   Feel self-pity
Ask other believers to stand with me
Other: _____

𝕻𝖗𝖆𝖞 . . .

Lord Jesus, You have already defeated the enemy. I claim victory over the enemy in Your name. Amen.

Day 13

Faith Without Love

And though I have all faith, so that I could remove mountains, and have not charity, I am nothing.

—1 Corinthians 13:2

Suppose I had *all faith so I could remove mountains, and I had a big farm but there was some of my farmland that was not very profitable. It was stony, had many rocks upon it, and some little mountains on it that were absolutely untillable and no good. But because I have faith without charity, I say, "I will use my faith, and I will move this land. I do not care where it goes so long as my land is clean." So I use my faith to clear my land.*

The next day my poor next-door neighbor comes and says, "I am in great trouble. All your wasteland and stony, rocky land has been tipped onto mine, and my good land is spoiled."

And I, who have faith without charity, say to him, "You get faith and move it back!" That profits nothing.[27]

When is faith not profitable? When it is exercised without *love* (charity). Think of a time when you were around a person who exercised his faith but was unloving. Answer these questions:

How were you treated by a person with faith who lacked love? _____

_____

How did you feel about that person? _____

_____

What was your response to that person? _____

_____

Faith must be exercised with unconditional love (*agape*) toward both God and others. James writes that faith without works is dead (James 2:26). We might amplify that to say that *faith without the work of love is dead.*

Paul describes unconditional, divine love (*agape*) in 1 Corinthians 13. When faith acts, each quality of love must be a part of faith. Below are the qualities of love that Paul lists. Examine yourself, and put an *x* on the line to indicate where you are right now, and a check to indicate where you should be:

My faith exercised in love is . . .

Patient _____ Impatient

Kind _____ Not kind

Accepting _____ Jealous

Humble _____ Proud

Polite _____ Rude

Selfless _____ Selfish

Slow to anger	Angers quickly

Rejoices in the good	Rejoices in wrong

Endures	Fails

Faith in Christ bears the fruit of love. Read the following passages, and write down what Jesus says about love:

John 15:9 _____

_____

John 15:10 _____

_____

John 15:12 _____

_____

John 15:13 _____

_____

John 15:17 _____

_____

Pray . . .

Lord, by the power of Your Spirit, bear the fruit of love in and through me whenever I exercise my faith in You. Amen.

Day 14

When Faith Is Tested

Therefore being justified by faith . . . we glory in tribulations also: knowing that tribulation worketh patience; and patience, experience.

—ROMANS 5:1, 3–4

COUNT IT ALL *joy in the midst of temptations. When the trial is severe, when you think that no one is tried as much as you, count it all joy. When you feel that some strange thing has so happened that you are altogether in a new order, count it all joy. When the trial is so hard you cannot sleep, count it all joy. God has something for you in the trial, something divine, something of a divine nature.*[28]

James assures us that our faith will be tested by fire and refined as pure gold (1 Pet. 1:7). Jesus instructs us that in this world we will have tribulations and trials (John 16:33). How do you respond when you face a trial or test? Check all that apply.

❑ I get angry.
❑ I become frustrated.
❑ I ask, "Why, God?"
❑ I complain.
❑ I rejoice.
❑ I seek God all the more.
❑ I grow spiritually.
❑ I resist the work God is trying to do in my life.

❏ I learn much from the trial about God and myself.
❏ I _____ .

A FTER ABRAHAM WAS *tried he could offer Isaac — not before he was tried. God put Abraham through all kinds of tests. For twenty-five years he was tested. He is called the "father of the faithful" because he would not give up when he was under trials. We have a blessing today because one man dared to believe God without moving away from Him for twenty-five years.*[29]

Abraham's love and trust for God were tried. If Abraham loved Isaac more than he loved and trusted God, he would have failed the test.

Describe a time when your love and trust in God were put to the test. How did you respond?

_____

_____

_____

_____

_____

When God put Abraham through his trial of faith with Isaac, God also provided a way to endure the trial. Read Genesis 22:10–14. Answer these questions:

What provision did God make for Abraham? _____

_____

How did Abraham respond to God's provision? _____

_____

What provision does God make for us in the midst of our trials? _____

_____

    If you had difficulty answering the last question, consider these provisions: salvation in Christ; power in the Holy Spirit; the intercession of the Spirit through us; the Word of God; the fellowship of the believers; and the encouragement of the body of Christ. All of these help us in times of trial.

Pray . . .

Lord Jesus, sustain me through every trial and strengthen my faith in every test. Amen.

Day 15

Ask and Believe

And all things, whatsoever ye shall ask in prayer, believing, ye shall receive.

—MATTHEW 21:22

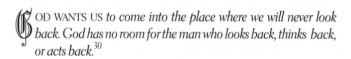

GOD WANTS US *to come into the place where we will never look back. God has no room for the man who looks back, thinks back, or acts back.*[30]

There is nothing to go back for! The past may be filled with failures, sin, and regrets. But for the believer, all of the past is covered by the blood of Jesus Christ.

God is doing a new thing in your life. He is moving ahead into His future. Will you go with God or remain chained to your past? Complete these sentences:

One thing that tempts me to look back is _____

_____ .

One thing that hinders me from going on with God is

_____ .

Surrender to God whatever tempts you to look back. Be loosed and set free from the past! John tells us that we can be set free to fellowship with the Lord and to move ahead with Him. Below is a paraphrased section of 1 John 1. Put your name in the blanks, and then read the text aloud:

The one who existed from the beginning is the one
_____ has heard and seen. _____ saw him
with _____ own eyes and touched him with
_____'s own hands. He is Jesus Christ, the Word
of life. This one who is life from God was shown to
_____, and _____ has seen him. And now
_____ testifies and announces to you that he is
the one who is eternal life. He was with the Father,
and then he was shown to _____. _____ is
telling you about what _____ has actually seen
and heard, so that you may have fellowship with
_____. And _____'s fellowship is with the
Father and with his Son, Jesus Christ.

_____ is writing these things so that
_____'s joy will be complete. This is the message
he has given us to announce to you: God is light and
there is no darkness in him at all. So _____ is
lying if _____ says _____ has fellowship
with God but goes on living in spiritual darkness.
_____ is not living in the truth. But if _____
is living in the light of God's presence, just as Christ
is, then we have fellowship with each other, and the
blood of Jesus, his Son, cleanses _____ from
every sin.

If _____ says that _____ has no sin,
_____ is only fooling (him/her)self and refusing
to accept the truth. But if _____ confesses
_____'s sins to him, he is faithful and just to for-
give _____ and to cleanse _____ from every
wrong. If _____ claims _____ has not
sinned, _____ is calling God a liar and showing
that his word has no place in _____'s heart
(NLT).

Confession sets you free from the past to live in God's freedom and liberty through faith in Christ.

THE HOLY GHOST *wants to get you ready for stretching yourself out to Him, believing that He is a rewarder of them that diligently seek Him. You need not use vain repetition. Ask and believe.*[31]

Write a prayer that truly asks and believes Jesus by faith for what you need:

_____

_____

_____

𝔓𝔯𝔞𝔶 . . .

Lord, release me from my past that I might be free to go with You into Your future. Amen.

Day 16

The Leap of Faith

Jesus saith unto her [Martha], Said I not unto thee, that, if thou wouldest believe, thou shouldest see the glory of God?

—JOHN 11:40

YOU HAVE TO *take a leap today. Leap into the promises. You have to believe that God never fails you—that it is impossible for God to break His Word. He is from everlasting to everlasting.*
Forever and ever, not for a day.
He keepeth His promise forever,
To all who believe, to all who obey,
He keepeth His promise forever.[32]

Make a list below of five ways that God has been faithful to you in the past.

God has been faithful in my finances to _____

_____.

God kept His promises to me in relationships by_____

_____.

God has been faithful in my needs to _____

_____.

God has kept His promise in my family to _____

_____.

God has shown His faithfulness to me through other believers in _____

_____.

Now read the following passages, and write down what each says about His promises to you:

2 Corinthians 1:20 _____

_____

Hebrews 6:12–20 _____

_____

Hebrews 8:6 _____

_____

2 Peter 1:4 _____

_____

HERE IS NO *variableness with God. There is no shadow of turning. He is the same. He manifests His divine glory. To Mary and Martha, Jesus said, "If thou wouldest believe, thou shouldest see the glory of God." He was tempted in all points, like as we, yet without sin. He endured all things. He is our example.*[33]

Consider all that Jesus did to fulfill the promises of God and to impart His life and glory to you. Read Philippians 2:5–8. List the seven things Jesus did for you to demonstrate His love for you:

1. _____
2. _____
3. _____
4. _____
5. _____
6. _____
7. _____

He is the same yesterday, today, and tomorrow (Heb. 13:8). Follow His example. Obey Him. He will open up all His blessings to you.

𝕻𝖗𝖆𝖞 . . .

Lord Jesus, help me to follow You and claim Your promises by faith every day. Grant me the courage to take the leap of faith. Amen.

Day 17

Faith Laughs at Impossibilities

Jesus said unto them . . . if ye have faith as a grain of
mustard seed . . . nothing shall be impossible unto you.
— MATTHEW 17:20

FOUR THINGS ARE *emblematic, divinely ascertained, or revealed*
by the Lord—fire, love, zeal, faith. Fire, burning up intensely,
making us full of activity on line with God. Love, where there is
nothing but pure, undefiled willingness, yieldedness, knowing no
sacrifice. Zeal, so in the will and the mighty power of God until we
press beyond measure into that which pleases God.[34]

God is the God of the impossible. Faith in Him ac-
complishes the impossible. Read the following verses,
and write down how God does the impossible:

Matthew 17:20 _____

_____

Matthew 19:26 _____

_____

Mark 10:27 _____

_____

Luke 1:37 _____

_____

Luke 17:1 _____

_____

Luke 18:27 _____

_____

Are you facing something impossible? How strong are your fire, love, and zeal? Examine yourself and put an *x* on the line that represents where you are now:

When facing the impossible, the fire within me for accomplishing all things through faith in Christ is:

_____
Very hot   Lukewarm   Cold

When facing the impossible, my love for Christ is:

_____
Passionate   Indifferent

When facing the impossible, my zeal for doing what Christ requires is:

_____
Intense   Waning

Faith opens the door for Holy Spirit's fire, passionate love for Christ, and intense zeal to accomplish anything He desires.

FAITH, THAT LAUGHS *at impossibilities, and cries, "It shall be done!"* [35]

When God brings you face to face with accomplishing an impossible task, what are your usual responses? Check all that apply.

- ❏ Excitement, zeal, and passion
- ❏ Greater love for Him
- ❏ Fired up to do what He desires
- ❏ Hesitant and cautious
- ❏ Fearful and reluctant
- ❏ Other: _____

Describe an impossible task that He is requiring you to do right now: _____

_____

_____

_____

Now speak the task aloud and cry out, "It *will* be done!" so that both you and the devil can hear your exclamation of faith.

Pray . . .

Lord Jesus, whatever You desire in my life will be done! Amen.

Day 18

Faith and the Atonement

And not only so, but we also joy in God through our Lord Jesus Christ, by whom we have now received the atonement.

—ROMANS 5:11

ATONEMENT IS *"at-one-ment."* *Perfect association is being at one in Christ. Whatever His appointment in the earth, whatever He was, we have been joined up to Him in "one-ment." The atonement is "one-ment," meaning that He has absolutely taken every vestige of human deformity, depravity, lack of comprehension, and inactivity of faith and has nailed it to the cross. It's forever on the cross. You died with Him on the cross. If you will only believe you are dead with Him, you are dead indeed to sin and alive to righteousness.*[36]

The life of faith is one of daily crucifixion. Yes, we die to self when we are born again. But daily we must yield and surrender totally to Him, refusing the temptation to follow any desire of the flesh. Read these scriptures, and then write what needs to be crucified in your life today (Rom. 12:1–2; Gal. 2:20, 5:16–21; 2 Tim. 3:2–4):

_____

_____

_____

_____

_____

HERE IS NOT *a vestige of human weakness in His righteousness. If I dare believe, then I am so in order with God's Son that He makes me perfect, at one with Him, no sin, no blemish, no failure, absolutely a perfect atonement till there isn't a vestige of weakness left. Dare you believe it? If you dare believe now, then oneness, purity, power, and eternal fact are working through you.*[37]

One with Christ, we have His righteousness at work in our lives. He empowers us to "cleanse ourselves from all filthiness of the flesh and spirit, perfecting holiness in the fear of God" (2 Cor. 7:1). What spiritual disciplines is the Holy Spirit strengthening in your life? Check the ones that are being strengthened, and circle the ones that are now boldly at work in you:

❏ Witnessing   ❏ Prayer
❏ Praise   ❏ Worship
❏ Giving   ❏ Servanthood
❏ Fasting   ❏ Discipling others
❏ Fellowshiping with Christians
❏ Other: _____

Pray . . .

Lord Jesus, daily I die to self and seek to be perfectly at one with You. Amen.

Day 19

Trusting an Extravagant God

Bless the Lord, O my soul: and all that is within me,
bless his holy name. Bless the Lord, O my soul, and
forget not all his benefits.

—PSALM 103:1–2

A S I SEE IT, *Scripture is extravagant. When God speaks to me,*
He says, "Anything you ask." When God is speaking of the
world's salvation, He says, "Whosoever believes." So I have an
extravagant God with extravagant language to make me an extrava-
gant person—in wisdom.[38]

How has the Lord extravagantly blessed your life?
Read Psalm 103, and then complete these sentences:

He forgives my iniquities—name them: _____

_____ .

He heals my diseases—name them: _____

_____ .

He redeems my life from destruction—how? _____

_____ .

He crowns me with lovingkindness—in what way? _____

_____ .

He crowns me with His mercies—how? _____

_____ .

He satisfies me with good things—what are they? _____

_____ .

He renews my youth—in what way? _____

_____ .

Remember to speak of His benefits aloud often so that you hear yourself praising God, and so that the enemy also hears your praise and flees.

YOU MUST LEARN *above all things that you have to be out, and God must be in you. The trouble with many people is that they never have gotten out so that He could get in. But if God ever gets in, you will be the first one out, never to come in anymore.*[39]

Have you fully gotten out of yourself? Have you abandoned and emptied self so that Jesus might fill you to overflowing with Himself? Have you been filled with the Holy Spirit (Eph. 5:18)?

Reflect on the following areas of your life, and then shade the graph to the level you are filled with Christ's Spirit:

	Full	*Half-Full*	*Empty*
Relationships			
Finances			
Spiritual Life			
Work			
Marriage or Family			

Full of Christ, there is no room for self. He is your all in all. Guard your senses, refusing to let anything of the world in, and only allow His words and actions out of your life.

Pray . . .

Lord Jesus, fill my life with You. I empty my life of self and the world. Be my all in all. Amen.

Day 20

Have a Real Faith

*Therefore whosoever heareth these sayings of mine,
and doeth them, I will liken him unto a wise man,
which built his house upon a rock.*

—MATTHEW 7:24

ARE YOU READY *to believe the Scriptures? The Scripture is our foundation to build upon properly.*[40]

The Word of God is the rock upon which we build our faith. Ignorance of the Word results in weak, superficial faith. Knowledge of His Word strengthens and empowers faith. Read Psalm 119, and then, on the Bible below, list ten reasons the Word is important for your life of faith.

C HRIST IS THE *cornerstone. We are all in the building.*[41]

Real faith is strengthened by fellowship with other Christians. We are not called to love and serve Christ alone. Solitary sheep get attacked and devoured by the enemy. Together we are a royal priesthood, a holy nation of God's people built on the rock of Christ (1 Pet. 2:5–10). List five believers with whom you fellowship and have accountability in the faith:

1. _____

2. _____

3. _____

4. _____

5. _____

Now write a prayer thanking Christ for these believers who are helping you to grow in faith. If you cannot list five, ask Christ to lead you to other believers who will help you to grow in faith.

_____

_____

_____

C LAIM YOUR RIGHTS *in God's order. Do not give way. Have a real faith. Believe that love covers you. His life flows through you. His quickening Spirit lifts you.*[42]

If we are ignorant of His Word, then we will be ignorant of our rights as believers. Our faith will be unreal and weak through a lack of knowledge.

Check all the ways you are feeding on His Word in your life:

❑ Daily Bible reading and study
❑ Listening regularly to preaching in services, through tapes, radio, or television
❑ Participating in a small group Bible Study
❑ Participating in Sunday school
❑ Taking Bible study courses
❑ Memorizing the Word
❑ Singing, praying, and meditating on the Word
❑ Other: _____

Pray . . .

Lord Jesus, keep me always in Your Word. Amen.

Day 21

Believing as a Son of God

But as many as received him, to them gave he power to become the sons of God, even to them that believe on his name.

—JOHN 1:12

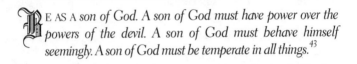

BE AS A *son of God. A son of God must have power over the powers of the devil. A son of God must behave himself seemingly. A son of God must be temperate in all things.*[43]

How does one become a son of God? What power does a believer receive as a son of God? Read the following verses, and write down the rights of a son of God:

John 1:12–13 _____

_____

Romans 8:14–19 _____

_____

Philippians 2:15 _____

_____

1 John 2:28–29 _____

_____

1 John 3:1–2 _____

_____

1 John 4:4–6 _____

_____

A SON OF GOD *must have the expression of the Master. He should be filled with tenderness and compassion. He should have a body filled with bowels of mercy. A son of God must excel in every way. God spoke and the heavens gave place to His voice. God proclaimed, "This is my beloved son . . . hear ye him" (Matt. 17:5). Afterward, Jesus always said, "I am the Son of God." God comes to you and says, "Behold, you are sons of God!" Oh, that we could have a regiment rising, claiming their rights, standing erect with a holy vision, and full of inward power, saying, "I am, by the grace of God, a son of God!"* [44]

You are being transformed into the likeness of Christ from glory to glory. Read 2 Corinthians 3:17–18, and rewrite the verses in your own words:

_____

_____

_____

What is the source of your power? The source is the Spirit of God and not your own power. Below are some verses that talk about the source of your power in faith. Write down what each verse says:

Zechariah 4:6 _____

_____

Acts 1:8 _____

_____

Ephesians 1:15–23 _____

_____

Ephesians 3:16–21 _____

_____

Philippians 4:13–19 _____

_____

𝔓𝔯𝔞𝔶 . . .

Lord Jesus, fill me with Your abundant power so that I might live mightily as Your child. Amen.

Day 22

Unwavering Faith

If any of you lack wisdom, let him ask of God . . . it shall be given him. But let him ask in faith, nothing wavering.

—JAMES 1:5–6

I AM SATISFIED *that God, who is the builder of divine order, never brings confusion in His order. If you want this divine order in your life, if you want wisdom, you have to come to God believing.*[45]

When you seek God in faith, do you approach Him in full confidence or with wavering and doubt? On a scale of 1 *(always)*, to 5 *(never)*, mark these statements about your faith:

I pray believing that my prayers are answered.

| 1 | 2 | 3 | 4 | 5 |

I pray without any doubt in my heart.

| 1 | 2 | 3 | 4 | 5 |

I pray with God's Word in my mind and mouth.

| 1 | 2 | 3 | 4 | 5 |

I pray with others who build my faith and speak no doubt.

| 1 | 2 | 3 | 4 | 5 |

Praying in faith means trusting God's Word in spite of your feelings, experience, past, or the world's advice. Do not look beyond the Word for the truth about God's promises for you. Trust *only* in His Word, and He will bring it to pass. *Only believe!*

OD DOES NOT *honor unbelief. He honors faith. For example, if you ask God once for healing, you will get it. But if you ask a thousand times a day till you forgot what you were asking, you're not asking in faith. If you would, ask God for your healing now, then begin praising Him. He never breaks His promise. You would go out perfect. "Only believe."* [46]

Begin praying in faith, trusting God for the little things in life. How can you trust Him to heal you of cancer or heart disease if you have not first trusted Him to heal your common cold or daily aches and pains? Begin trusting Him now to work in the daily experiences of your life. Start with a mustard-seed faith for little things, and watch God grow your faith to trust Him for big things in life.

Below is a tree representing trusting God for the big things in your life. Beside the tree, write all the big things you need to surrender in faith to Him:

_____

_____

_____

_____

_____

Pray . . .

Lord, teach me to trust You for the little miracles each day so that I may know how to trust You for mighty signs and wonders. Amen.

Day 23

Precious Faith

To them that have obtained like precious faith with us through the righteousness of God and our Saviour Jesus Christ.

—2 PETER 1:1

AITH IN JESUS Christ gives us access to the fullness of God. It was by grace first. You were saved through grace. But now we have another grace, a grace of access; a grace of entering in; a grace of understanding the unfolding of the mystery; a grace which shall bring us into a place of the knowledge of God. All that the Father has, all that Jesus has, all the Holy Ghost has, we have access into.[47]

Consider all the treasures you have by faith in Christ Jesus. Below is a treasure chest filled with gems representing that precious faith. Read Ephesians 1 and 2. Write on the treasure chest all the precious gems you have received through Christ:

_____

_____

_____

_____

_____

_____

_____

E HAVE THE *right and an open door into all that God has for us. There is nothing that can keep us out. Jesus Christ is the Alpha and Omega for us, that we may know grace, favor, and mercy to lift us into and take us through. "Grace and peace be multiplied unto you through the knowledge of God, and of Jesus our Lord" (2 Pet. 1:2). You want grace multiplied? You want peace multiplied? You have it here if you dare to believe. We have access to the Father by faith through His grace.*[48]

Faith multiplies grace and peace in your life. How is Christ increasing His grace and peace within you? Check the areas where you are experiencing more grace and peace from Christ:

❏ Loving people who hurt me
❏ Forgiving others
❏ Being more patient
❏ Making wise and right decisions
❏ Being gracious to those who attack me
❏ Facing trials and tests of my faith

𝔓𝔯𝔞𝔶 . . .

Jesus, You are my grace and peace in life. Fill me more and more each day with Your Spirit. Amen.

Day 24

Rest in Faith

For we which have believed do enter into rest.

—HEBREWS 4:3

HEN THE DIVINE *has the full control, then all earthly cares and anxieties pass away. If we live in the Spirit, we are over all human nature. If we reach the climax God's Son said we had to come into, we shall always be in the place of peace. Jesus said, "If ye abide in me, and my words abide in you, ye shall ask what ye will, and it shall be done unto you" (John 15:7).*[49]

Are you abiding in His peace? Examine your life at the present moment. Are you experiencing genuine peace and rest in Christ? Circle the following feelings that you have now:

Anxiety	Worry	Frustration
Depression	Anger	Despair
Hurt	Bitterness	Pain
Grief		
Other: _____		

If you circled none of the feelings listed above, or just one, then Christ's peace is taking control of your life. But if you found yourself having a number of negative feelings, then you need to surrender those feelings to Him in faith. If you did not circle any of the above feelings, then begin to praise Him for His rest and peace reigning in your life.

JESUS WAS THE *manifestation of power to dethrone every evil thing. He always dealt with the flesh. It was necessary for Him to say to Peter, "Get thee behind me, Satan: for thou savourest not the things that be of God, but the things that be of men" (Mark 8:33). Everything that interferes with your plan of putting to death the old man is surely the old man comforting you, so that you will not act to crucify the flesh. It is a rest in faith, a place where you can smile in the face of any eruption. No matter what comes, you will be in the place of real rest. (Matt. 11:28–29).*[50]

Genuine rest is available to every believer through faith. Your faith does not strive with principalities and powers of this world (Eph. 6:12). Rather, we put on His armor and rest in Him—He has already won the victory in His death and resurrection. Read the following scriptures, and jot down how His rest, joy, and peace are available to you:

Psalm 23 _____

_____

Psalm 91 _____

_____

Isaiah 61 _____

_____

Matthew 6 _____

_____

Philippians 4 _____

_____

Pray . . .

Lord Jesus, keep me from fighting battles You have already won. Fill me with Your rest, joy, and peace. Amen.

Day 25

One Faith

*There is one body, and one Spirit . . . One Lord, one
faith, one baptism, one God and Father of all, who is
above all, and through all, and in you all.*
—EPHESIANS 4:4–5

J UST IN THE *proportion that you have the Spirit unfolding to
you —* "One Lord, one faith, one baptism" *— you have the Holy
Ghost so incarnated in you, bringing into you a revelation of the
Word. Nothing else can do it, for the Spirit gave the Word through
Jesus. Jesus spoke by the Spirit that was in Him, being the Word. The
Spirit brought out all the Word of Life. Then we must have the Spirit.*[51]

In the body of Christ, we must have a unity of faith.
Satan seeks to divide the body over issues of dogma and
tradition. Read what Jesus said about such division in
Mark 7:13, and rewrite that verse in your own words:

_____

_____

_____

Paul wrote about the unity of faith in Christ we must
have in the church. Read 1 Corinthians 3, and then
answer the following questions:

What was causing division in the church at Corinth?

What is the foundation they were supposed to be building upon?

How do pride and the glory of men affect the church?

To whom does every person in the church belong?

There is no unity in the faith within the body of Christ outside of the one faith in Jesus Christ. How is the unity of faith in Christ manifesting itself in your church? Check everything that is happening:

❏ We pray in one accord and in unity.
❏ We worship in unity.
❏ We make decisions in unity.
❏ We witness in unity with other believers.
❏ We build one another up and do not tear one another down.
❏ We love one another as Christ loves us.
❏ We accept and affirm one another.
❏ Other:

T HE CHURCH WILL *rise to the highest position when there is no schism in the body on the lines of unbelief. When we all with one heart and one faith believe the Word as it is spoken, then signs, wonders, and various kinds of miracles will be manifested. There will be one accord, in "One Lord, one faith, one baptism." Hallelujah!* [52]

Read John 17, and then write your own prayer for unity of faith in Christ for your church:

_____

_____

_____

Pray . . .

Lord Jesus, unite all believers in love and faith so that they may be one in You. Amen.

Day 26

Holy Faith

But ye, beloved, building up yourselves on your most holy faith, praying in the Holy Ghost, keep yourselves in the love of God.

—JUDE 1:20–21

I SAW ONE *day a great big magnet let down amongst iron, and it picked up loads of iron and carried them away. That is a natural order, but ours is a spiritual order of a holy magnet. That which is in thee is holy. That which is in thee is pure. When the Lord of righteousness shall appear, who is our life, then that which is holy, which is His nature, which is His life, shall go, and we shall be forever with the Lord.*[53]

Trusting Christ puts us in a position of sanctification—being made holy. We are set apart as holy vessels to be used according to His will. Read the following scriptures, and write down how you are being sanctified:

John 17:17–19 _____

_____

1 Corinthians 1:30 _____

_____

Ephesians 5:26 _____

_____

1 Thessalonians 4:3, 5:23 _____

_____

2 Thessalonians 2:13 _____

_____

Hebrews 13:12 _____

_____

1 Peter 1:2; 3:15 _____

_____

SK GOD THAT *every moment shall be a moment of purifying, a moment of raptureseeking, a moment in your body of a new order of the Spirit. Let God take you into the fullness of redemption in a wonderful way. Covet to be more holy. Covet to be more separate. Covet God. Covet holy faith.*[54]

Faith in Christ produces the fruit of holiness in our lives. As we trust Him, He sanctifies us. Read the following verses, and then summarize the desire that God has for our holiness (Rom. 6:22; 2 Cor. 7:1; Eph. 4:24; 1 Thess. 3:13, 4:7; 1 Tim. 2:15; Heb. 12:10–14):

_____

_____

_____

Pray . . .

Lord Jesus, bear Your fruit of holiness in my life. Amen.

Day 27

Faith That Trusts

And such trust have we through Christ to God-ward:
Not that we are sufficient of ourselves to think any
thing as of ourselves; but our sufficiency is of God.
—2 CORINTHIANS 3:4–5

WE WANT TO *get to a place where we are beyond trusting*
ourselves. Beloved, there is so much failure in self assurances. It
is not bad to have good things on the lines of satisfaction, but
we must never have anything on the human plane that we rest upon.
There is only one sure place to rest upon, and our trust is in God. In
Thy name we go. In Thee we trust. And God brings us off in victory.
When we have no confidence in ourselves to trust in our God, He has
promised to be with us at all times, to make the path straight, and to
make a way. Then we understand how it is that David could say, "Thy
gentleness hath made me great" (2 Sam. 22:36).[55]

True faith moves from a life preserver to the lifesaver.
What does this mean? A life preserver is something that
we hold onto with all of our strength. But if no lifesaver
came to our rescue, eventually our strength would fail,
and we would be lost. A lifesaver is a person who comes
to rescue us. They take us from danger to safety, from
deep water to dry ground, and from near death to life.
Everything in life is merely a life preserver. Only Jesus is
a lifesaver. So then faith moves us from a life preserver to
the lifesaver.

Below is a life preserver. What are some of the things that you often try to hold onto to and trust just to survive? For example, money, people, career, etc. Write the most important life preservers to you on the picture below.

AH, THOU LOVER *of souls! We have no confidence in the flesh. Our confidence can only stand and rely on the One who is able to come in at the midnight hour as easily as at noonday and make the night and the day alike to the man who rests completely in the will of God, knowing that "all things work together for good to them that love God," and trust Him. And such trust have we in Him. The Lord has helped me to have no confidence in myself but to trust wholly in Him, bless His name!* [56]

Our confidence and trust is totally in Jesus Christ. Read the following verses, and write down how your trust in Christ is grounded in total confidence:

Psalm 27:1–3 _____

_____

Psalm 118:8–9

Proverbs 3:26, 14:26

2 Corinthians 5:6–8

Ephesians 3:11–12

Philippians 1:6

Hebrews 3:6, 14

1 John 3:21, 5:14

Are you trusting in a life preserver or in the Lifesaver? Is your confidence in your own ability or in the Lord?

Pray . . .

Lord, in You alone I place my trust and my confidence. Amen.

Day 28

Faith Lets Go

*Let us lay aside every weight, and the sin which doth
so easily beset us . . . Looking unto Jesus the author
and finisher of our faith.*

—HEBREWS 12:1–2

HOW MAY I get nearer to God? How may I be in the place of help-lessness in my own place and dependent on God?[57]

In order to grasp God, you must let go of anything or
anyone you are holding onto other than God (Acts
17:27–28). He is not far off from those who seek Him by
faith. So when we draw close to Him, He will draw near
to us (James 4:8). What do you need to let go of in order
to draw near to and grasp the presence of God in your
life? Check all that apply.

- ❏ Pride
- ❏ Religious tradition
- ❏ Work or career
- ❏ Unconfessed sin
- ❏ Other: _____

- ❏ Busyness
- ❏ Money
- ❏ Fear
- ❏ Insecurity

ET YOURSELF GO till He is on the throne. Let everything submit itself to the throne and the King. If you will let go, God will take hold and keep you up. Oh, to seek only the will of God, to be only in the purpose of God, to seek only that God shall be glorified, not I![58]

Faith puts Christ as Lord and King on the throne of your life. Since God is a jealous God, He will not share that throne with anyone or anything else. Read the story of the rich young ruler (Matt. 19:16–30; Mark 10:17–22; Luke 18:18–30), and answer the following questions:

What was the young man seeking? _____

_____

What was on the throne of his life? _____

_____

What did Jesus require of him? _____

_____

Why couldn't he obey Jesus? _____

_____

Write a prayer asking Jesus to take sole possession of the throne in your life:

_____

Pray . . .

Jesus, You are my Lord and my King. I desire to draw near to You and to stay continually in Your presence. Amen.

Day 29

Faith and Grace

Therefore it is of faith, that it might be by grace; to the end the promise might be sure to all the seed.

—ROMANS 4:16

G OD'S WORD SAYS, *"By faith, that it may be by grace."* Grace is omnipotent, active, benevolent, and merciful. Grace is true, perfect, and an inheritance from God that the soul can believe. Grace is of God. It is by faith. You open the door by faith, and God comes in with all you want.[59]

Faith makes us receptive to receive the free gift of God—grace in Christ. Grace is not what we earn but what we receive in Jesus. Think of all that you have received freely in Jesus. On the gift below, write some of the ways you have experienced God's grace in your life:

AITH ACTS ON *a fact. A fact brings joy. So you hear the Scriptures, which make you wise unto salvation, opening your understanding, so that if you hear the truth and believe, you will receive what you want. By faith you open and shut the door. By grace, God comes in — saving, healing, and meeting your needs.*[60]

Faith opens the door of your life to receive the healing and liberating anointing of Jesus Christ. Read Luke 4:16–19. In your own words, describe how placing your trust in Jesus has enabled Him to save you, heal you, and set you free.

_____

_____

_____

Pray . . .

Jesus, thank You for setting me free because I am trusting in You as my Lord and Savior. Amen.

Day 30

Living Faith

That your faith should not stand in the wisdom of men, but in the power of God.

—1 CORINTHIANS 2:5

FAITH HAS THE *power of access. Living faith is unfeigned faith, faith that never wavers. Faith comes from the Author of faith. By a living faith in God, the crooked are made straight, the lame leap with joy, and the blind are made free.*[61]

Faith in Jesus gives you access to the throne of God. Living faith is a living relationship with Christ that lasts forever. As you reflect on this study of faith, complete the following sentences:

A living faith in Christ is _____

_____ .

To trust Him totally, I have totally surrendered _____

_____ .

The most insightful thing I have learned about faith is

_____ .

One way I feel closer to the Lord after this study is _____

_____ .

One way my faith has grown is _____

_____ .

I need to grow in faith by _____

_____ .

Write a prayer telling Jesus that you trust Him completely:

_____

_____

_____

𝕻𝖗𝖆𝖞 . . .

Lord Jesus, I surrender all to You in faith. Amen.

Leader's Guide

For Group Sessions

This devotional study is an excellent resource for group study including such settings as:

- ❖ Sunday school classes and other church classes.
- ❖ Prayer groups.
- ❖ Bible study groups.
- ❖ Ministries involving small groups, home groups, and accountability groups.
- ❖ Study groups for youth and adults.

Before the first session

- ❖ Contact everyone interested or already participating in the group about the meeting time, date, and place.
- ❖ Make certain that everyone has a copy of this devotional study guide, *The Original Smith Wigglesworth Devotional,* and the *Holy Spirit Encounter Bible.*
- ❖ Ask group members to begin their daily encounters in this guide. Plan for six sessions with each group session covering five devotional studies. Group members who faithfully complete a devotional each day will be prepared to share in the group sessions. Plan out all your sessions before starting the first session.
- ❖ Pray for the Holy Spirit to guide, teach, and help each participant.
- ❖ Be certain that the place where you will meet has a chalkboard, white board, or flip chart with

appropriate writing materials. It is also best to be in a setting with movable, not fixed, seating.

Planning the Group Sessions

1. You will have six sessions together as a group. Plan to cover at least five days in each session.

2. In your first session, allow group members to select a partner with whom they will share and pray during each session. Keep the same pairs together throughout the group sessions. You can put pairs together randomly—men with men and women with women.

3. Begin each session with prayer.

4. Read or ask group members to read the key scriptures at the start of each daily devotional for the five days prior to that session.

5. Prior to each session, decide which exercises and questions you would like to cover from the five daily devotional studies for that session.

6. Decide which exercises and sessions will be most appropriate for your group to share as a whole and which would be more comfortable for group members to share in pairs.

7. From the five previous days, decide which prayer(s) you wish the pairs to pray with one another.

8. Close each session with each group member sharing with the total group how he or she grew in faith during the previous week. Then lead the group in prayer, or have group members pray aloud. Close the session with your own prayer.

9. In the last session, use the thirtieth day as an in-depth sharing time in pairs. Invite all the

group members to share the most important thing they learned about faith during this study, and how their relationship with the Lord was deepened during the study. Close with prayers of praise and thanksgiving.

10. Whether sharing in pairs or as a total group, remember to allow each person the freedom not to share if they are not comfortable.

11. Be careful—this is not a therapy group. Group members who seek to dominate group discussions with their own problems or questions should be ministered to by the group leader or pastor in a one-on-one setting outside of the group session.

12. Always start and end the group session on time, and seek to keep the session within a ninety-minute time frame.

Notes

All resources by Smith Wigglesworth may be found in the archives of the Assemblies of God headquarters in Springfield, Missouri. We express our appreciation to the archives and its staff for the privilege of researching these materials.

1. "Faith (Part Two)," message presented at Glad Tidings Tabernacle, 3 August 1922, 1.
2. Ibid.
3. Ibid.
4. "Believe! The Way to Overcome," Faith Leaflet No. 1.
5. Ibid.
6. Ibid.
7. "Sons of God," Bible study no. 7, 14 July 1927, 4.
8. Ibid.
9. "Overcoming," message preached in Berkeley, CA,. 3 June 1924, 5.
10. Ibid.
11. "Faith (Part Two)," message presented at Glad Tidings Tabernacle, 3 August 1922, 3.
12. Ibid., 1.
13. "Rising Into the Heavenlies," address presented in Wellington, New Zealand, 24 January 1924, 8–9.
14. Ibid.
15. "Now! Now! Now!," message presented in Colombier, Switzerland, n.d., 2–3.
16. Ibid.
17. An untitled address presented at the Bethany Pentecostal Mission Room, Pudsey, 5 September 1925, 1–2.
18. Ibid.
19. "Floodtide, Faith Leaflet No. 2, 3–4.
20. Ibid.
21. "Faith (Part Two)," message presented at Glad Tidings Tabernacle, 3 August 1922, 5.
22. Ibid.
23. "That I May Know Him," message presented at Glad Tidings Tabernacle, 20 August 1922, 4–5.
24. Ibid.
25. "Ephesians 4:1–16," Bible study no. 9, 19 July 1927, 10.

26. Ibid.
27. Bible study no. 8, 15 July 1927, 8–9.
28. "Temptation Endured," Bible study no. 12, 22 July 1927, 3.
29. Ibid.
30. "Workers Together With God," Bible study no. 15, 28 July 1927, 1.
31. Ibid.
32. "Temptation Endured," Bible study no. 12, 22 July 1927, 5.
33. Ibid.
34. "This Grace," Bible study no. 26, 19 August 1927, 1.
35. Ibid.
36. "This Grace," Bible study no. 26, 19 August 1927, 7.
37. Ibid.
38. "God Bless You!," Bible study no. 4, 8 July 1927, 6.
39. Ibid.
40. "Workers Together With God," Bible study no. 15, 28 July 1927, 14.
41. Ibid.
42. Ibid.
43. "Sons of God," Bible study no. 7, 14 July 1927, 7.
44. Ibid.
45. "Temptation Endured," Bible study no. 12, 22 July 1927, 10–11.
46. Ibid.
47. "This Grace," Bible study no. 26, 19 August 1927, 3.
48. Ibid.
49. "2 Corinthians 3," Bible study no. 16, 29 July 1927, 2.
50. Ibid.
51. "Our Calling (Part Two)," message presented at Glad Tidings Tabernacle, 22 August 1922, 5.
52. Ibid.
53. "This Grace," Bible study no. 26, 19 August 1927, 13.
54. Ibid.
55. "Ye Are Our Epistle (Part One)," message presented at Glad Tidings Tabernacle, 23 August 1922, 3.
56. Ibid.
57. "The Riches of His Glory," Bible study no. 14, 27 July 1927, 12.
58. Ibid.
59. "Faith," message at Good News Hall, Melbourne, Australia, 1922, 3.
60. Ibid.
61. Ibid.